THIS BOOK

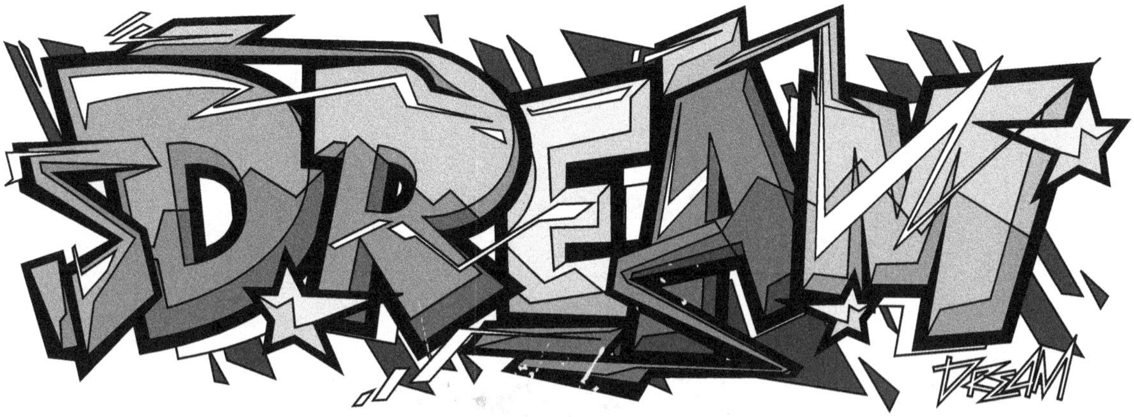

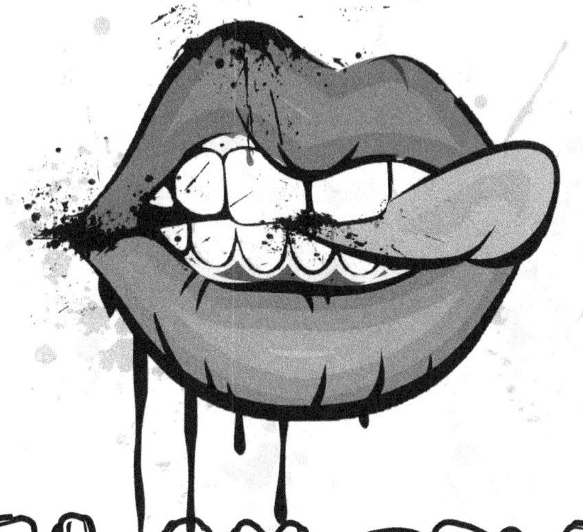

BELONGS TO:

_ _ _ _ _ _ _ _ _ _ _ _ _ _ _

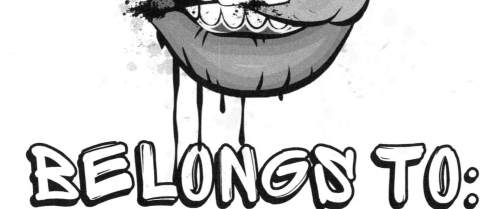

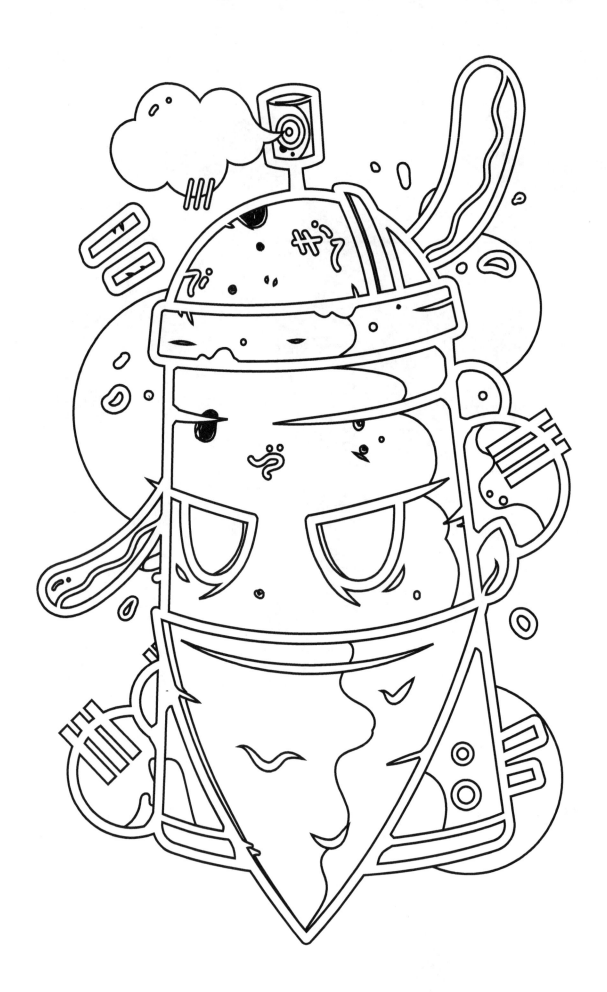

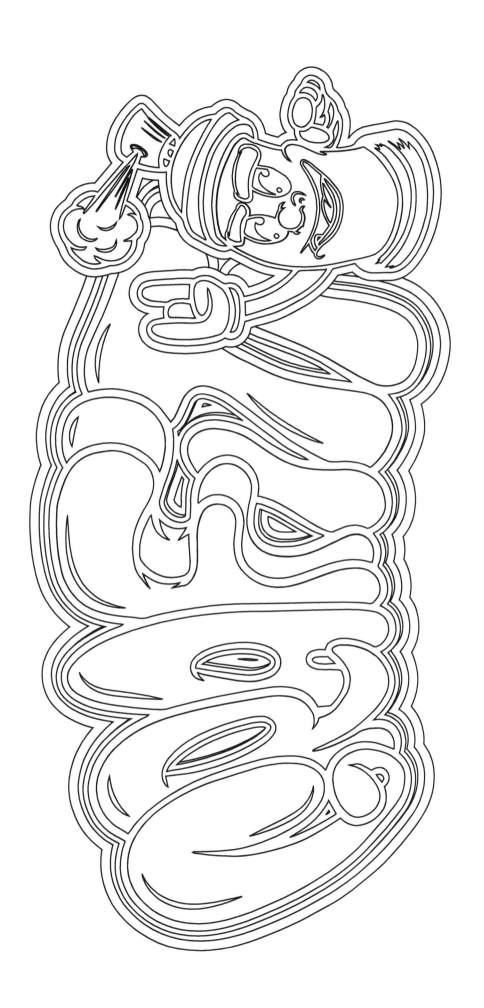

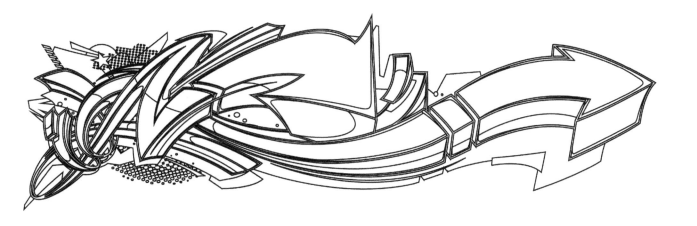

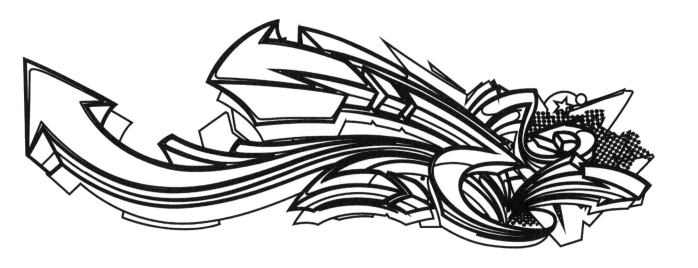

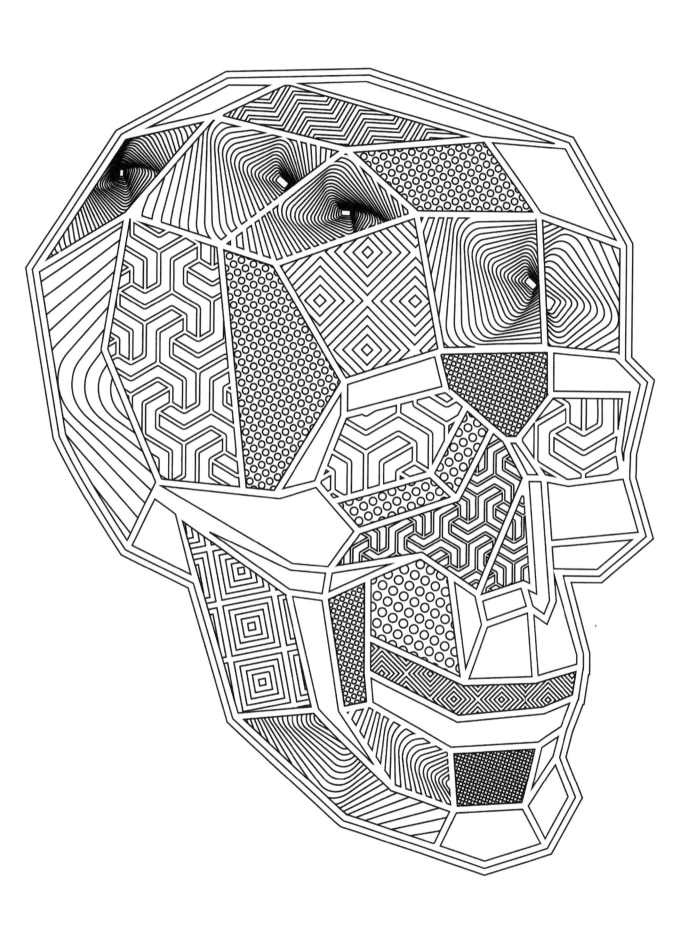

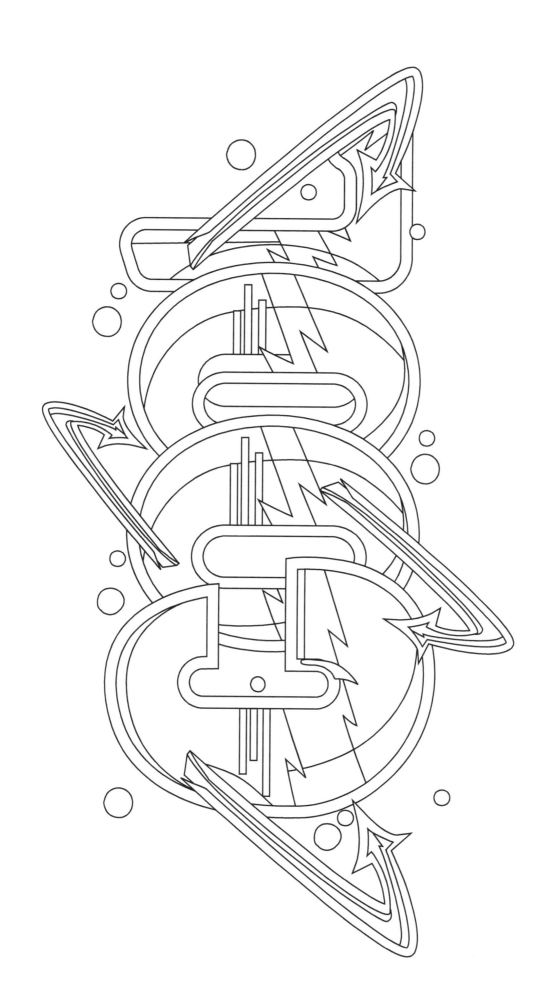

Thank you for your purchase, if you like the product, please don't forget to give me a review on my amazon product page

CPSIA information can be obtained
at www.ICGtesting.com
Printed in the USA
LVHW060823250323
742590LV00014B/517